Poems from Grace Cottage

Poems from Grace Cottage

To Christine with best wishes from Patricia Huth Ellis 2009.

Patricia Huth Ellis

THE WYCHWOOD PRESS

Wychwood Press books may be ordered from bookshops or (post free) from
Evenlode Books, Alder House, Market Street, Charlbury, OX7 3PH
01608 811969

e-mail: wychwood@joncarpenter.co.uk

Credit card orders should be phoned or faxed to 01689 870437 or 01608 811969

Published in 2006 by
The Wychwood Press
an imprint of Jon Carpenter Publishing
Alder House, Market Street, Charlbury, Oxfordshire OX7 3PH

ISBN 1 902279 25 5

Manufactured in the UK by LPPS Ltd, Wellingborough, Northants NN8 3PJ

For Geoffrey
with thanks and love

Acknowledgements

Publications

I am grateful to the editors of the following publications where several of these poems first appeared:
Acorn, The Lady, Second Light, The Charlbury Chronicle, Envoi, The Spectator.

Thanks

I should like to thank Antony Fernandez for his incredible patience and help in teaching me to use a computer. And I should like to thank also my fellow poets from Ewart House, Oxford, the Isis Poetry Group, and Suzy Ellis, for constant encouragement and help.

The cover picture of Grace Cottage is by Susan Woolley.

Table of Contents

Acknowledgement

We walked along the woodland path
my grandchild and I
noting nature things,
pointing out early primroses, aconites, wild violets.

We crossed the stream, and headed up the hill,
"Look a rabbit", my grandchild said.
Together we saw one magpie, then two.
We shared a chocolate bar, drank from the stream
cupping our hands.

Kneeling in the rich earth I said,
"we are part of this
you and I, dear granddaughter,
part of this earth is us".

She nodded.

"Do you know Grandpa, Granny?" she said.
"He said nature is part of us, or ought to be".
She chattered on and
God forgive me, I didn't hear.

Do I know Grandpa? Yes. A bit.
We lived together for twenty years,
I do know of his love for wild things,
for nature, and of his quick eye,
and how he loved me once
and how I loved him.

Yes, dear granddaughter,
I do know Grandpa.

My house

I left the house,

that housed me,
shelled me,
held me,
a house I loved.

I left the house,
with it peace there,
its space there,
its pace there,
a house I loved.

I left the house.

It is hard to think,
to breathe, to see,
the house I left
was part of me.

I loved the house,
the house I left,
that housed me,
shelled me,
held me.

I am bereft.

Que reste-t-il de nos amours?

A kitchen somewhere in France,
a candle alight on a small round table
remains of supper not yet cleared,
two old women sitting silently,
listening to soft music.

"Que reste-t-il de nos amours?
Que reste-t-il de ces beaux jours?"

The two old women rise slowly,
start to dance,
gently holding each other close
crumpled hand in crumpled hand,
cheek brushing cheek,
no words spoken.

Is it of the once vibrant love
they had had together
that they are thinking,
or of other loves, or that life is short,
and each of us only have one turn at it,
that life is only made of moments
and they have had their share?

"Que reste-t-il de tout cela?
Dites-le-moi".

The two old women dance on,
quietly swaying,
to soft music no longer playing.......

Safe Harbour

Old love settles for a safe harbour,
a place of quiet embracing
rocked in a gentle sea.

Young love is daring, dangerous,
rich in its fullness,
sticky in substance, ripe with seed.

Old love has a slower pace,
enriched with years of touch.
No need to preen and strut the hour.

The rib cage joins,
the bone becomes one bone,
the breath one breath.
Calm waters still seduce.

Not Patrick

The woman forgot
to say goodnight.
No footsteps on the stone,
dark passages silent,
her child's cries unheard.
A wet pillow, a wet bear
bore witness.

The woman loved men,
all men were gin in her tonic,
men for dazzle and dancing.
Uncles abounded, bringing presents
in exchange for loitering in the garden,
freeing the house for abandon.

The woman said the fault
was in the gender,
fate slipped up,
daughters were not expected.
She yearned for a son
to delight and love her,
understand her frailties.
Sons would have adorned her.

The woman, dying, summoned the priest
succumbed to the last rites,
gave up of herself to this last man.
There were no footsteps by the bed,
her last cries unheard,
no tears were shed.

Resolution

I need to breathe salt sea air,
run down the shell-strewn beach,
let the sharp east wind blow through my hair,
run for the horizon away out of reach.

I need the sound of the seagull's cry,
the music of waves rolling on sand
to help with questions of whether and why
I should change my direction, and stand

up for what I believe in.
I need the strength I know I will find
on that quiet sunfilled beach,
to be resolute, make up my mind.

Enveloped in peace, silence and sea
I will whisper to the listening wind,
"I have made the decision, watch over me,
I'm taking the path I've determined".

The House

Was it the sound of Chopin
filling the street air,
escaping from a large keyhole
in the weathered front door,
or the first glimpse of pale
stone flooring and a rocking horse
in the hall corner, or was it the
Easter lilies rising tall out of
white enamel jugs, and books
everywhere, everywhere?

Was it the ancient dog
in front of a small log fire,
protected by a staunch Victorian fireguard,
or the scrubbed table and gentian-blue
hyacinths peeking out of a copper bowl,
Rockingham pottery plates
each one different,
or the sculpture of an unknown woman
young, rounded smooth,
placed lovingly on a window shelf
catching a flicker of the January sun?

Or was it the smell of beef stew,
a nursery smell dredged from childhood,
or the sight of home-grown pears
floating in sugared juice?
Or was it the feeling of safety,
warmth and love
everywhere, everywhere
that overwhelmed me?

Inheritance

What was it that made me
think of you, who
are bone-dust now,
with no statue or monument
to bear your witness?
Was it the apple-bruised spots
on the Gloucester Old Spot pigs,
their legacy from apple orchards, long ago,
to mark them out?

In the afternoon sunlight
as I bent to touch their skin
I saw that my hands, brown-spotted,
were your hands, identical.
Was this your legacy to me,
something to say that you were here?

More precious than possessions,
you passed to me our inheritance
from some ancient eastern shore.
Your brownness, your hands, brown spotted,
which marked you.

January Weather

We know from recorded history,
that in St. Merryn
a hundred years ago,
there blew great winds
and the sea was smoking white.

We know it was warm in Kent,
where the thrushes thought spring
had come, and piped away.
And primroses were a yellow carpet
in North Norfolk,
or so the parson wrote.

We know of cutting winds in Hampshire,
of icicles and frost, and
in Skiddaw on a mild day,
a brown spotted butterfly was seen.
We know that hungry church
mice ate bible markers,
hungry people died of cold.

And we know that this dark winter month
had days of snow, that wild clouds
gathered in the sky unleashing icy rain,
churning up the plough.

And yet, again, we also know
the sun shone in that distant year,
it was warm enough to push through
early snowdrops, and Holy Thorn.
Light was glimpsed, here and there,
all life struggled for its moments.

Love Unlocked

What can I say about love
that has not been said?

I have little to add except
my sweetheart proffered
a unique key
to the door of possibilities,
through loving me.

No Whispered Warning

Catlin skips to school,
October leaves, red and yellow
fall across her path,
but do not whisper
warnings in her ear.

At breaktime Morwena falls
playing tag, and the children laugh.
All at once, from the valley,
an ominous noise,
engulfs the happy playground sounds,
as the derelict monster slagheap
starts to slip, slowly at first,
then gathering speed,
faster, faster, faster.

The blue sky blackens,
the mountain of dross,
cinders and mud,
rolls and trembles and shifts
as the angry giant roars,
burying the village school
under countless tons of coal.

Dust hangs in the air,
and silence, and more silence
then screams, and more screams,
tears and disbelief;
and the leaves, red and yellow,
still papering the ground.

Presents

I don't want presents
tied and ribboned.
Encouragement doesn't wrap
well in green tissue,
praise in paisley boxes
or love in thick gold paper.
I don't want guilt
compressed into an envelope,
with cheque.

A parcel of thoughtfulness,
a parcel of interest,
a parcel of embracing,
a parcel of safety, were
the presents I hoped for
under the festive tree.
The presents I hoped for
which were not to be.

Quickening

I want the pulse of life that has been asleep
to wake, embrace me, put on the light.
To hear the thrush, song-repeat, to keep
my trust in God to hurry icy winter's flight.
I want to glimpse, under sodden leaves, green shoots
to announce life's circle, its beginnings, have begun.
I want to run barefoot, abandon boots,
to walk through primrose paths, savour the sun.
I want to take off winter's dress, change its season,
to see the coloured petticoats of spring, bloom
and show us mortals nature's reason
to start afresh, admire the peacock's plume.
Cellar the coal, brush the ashes from the fire,
I want to intertwine, my love, quicken, feel desire.

Ramparts

To keep people out,
medieval man built castle walls,
dug moats, constructed drawbridges.
"No admission" was understood
from oaken doors, black studded.

Modern man spoils streets,
violates the countryside
with "keep out" signs.
Things do not change.

Ramparts encircle people.
"No admission" written on faces,
and "looks" are sent with
a private label.

These rejections, solid or implied
do not threaten me,
"Keep out" outdared by my skylark spirit.
It flies free.

Separation

Sometimes, in the night, sharing our bed
I feel cage-restrained.
I cannot stretch, or scratch, or swear
at moths or mosquitoes looking for
the light, or me. I cannot listen to the
World Service, speak out loud or hum.

And yet and yet, separated,
my being yearns for you.
Not for rapturous couplings
not for passion, but for oneness.
It is my primordial need
to share the beat of breath,
the silent, unconscious rhythm of life
that is not yet death.

Miracle

Rich in England's spring,
cowparsley entrancing
in dog-rosed hedge,
the fecund earth lush green,
a baby swallow
hatches in a Suffolk barn,
to the cries of gulls
flying over mudflats,
over sea-lavender.

This small bird grows
embracing our summer warmth,
swooping on insects caught
above rolling grasslands.
It dips and tumbles gracefully,
trouble-free.

But what instinct tells of winter's cold?
This bird, hand-sized, will
fly over icy Pyrenees,
thirst through the parched Sahara,
soar and glide on trade winds,
south to The Cape of Africa
drawn, inexplicably, to the heat
of the southern sun.

In early spring does
this swallow's courageous heart
grow restless, homesick for
a Suffolk barn?
Is it a miracle that some force
of nature returns this minute bird
to its birth-nest by the English sea?
Who knows, but it seems so to me.

The Man from Middlesbrough

ordered another cup of tea,
lit another cigarette.

He held his head
in his history-stained hands,
nicotine fingers clutching
tufts of dirty grey hair.
He stared, not-seeing, at
the plastic tablecloth,
his mind numb.

His father, his grandfather,
worked in this shipyard
watched ships lovingly grow
from steel plates to proud traders,
built to sail from the Tees estuary,
into the North Sea
and the world's great oceans.

In his head the man heard the noise,
music to him, of drag chains,
when a ship pushed along
the greasy slipway, slid into the sea.
And the man thought of his mates,
of shared experiences from schooldays,
first girlfriends, first kisses,
walks in the Cleveland hills.
And he thought of the old canteen,
warm with steam from the tea urn,
from brotherhood.

The man wiped his eyes
with the back of his hand,

ordered another cup of tea,
lit another cigarette.

Screams Unheard

It is very well done, she said,
the War Museum,
we will visit one afternoon.
Visit the dead?
I know the grief and loss wars cause,
I remain silent, pause
then say, yes why not.

We did visit,
people crowded everywhere.
Schoolchildren were
chewing gum, shouting,
scribbling on odd pieces of paper,
bored with the uncool dead,
and old history.

We lunched in the restaurant
on hot soup, buttered buns,
then hurried downstairs to
inspect tanks and guns.
Under lowered lights
in ominous gloom,
sepia scenes of uniformed men
hung in a darkened room.

Underground now,
the bowels of the earth.
Ah, the virtual reality attraction
the gas chamber.
Permission to touch
the white tiles, the copper pipes
where the gas would come
not very nice, but very well done.

A teenager laughed,
licked his ice cream,
then wandered away,
obscene, obscene.

Normandy landings next
on film,
Sea-sodden soldiers, exhausted, cold,
weary young faces, made old,
blasts of noise, terror and blood,
bulleted corpses floating in mud.
Screech, more aircraft over,
some of "our boys" after the Hun.
Very clever, very real,
very well done.

We should have gone to the Dolls
Museum, she said.
Perhaps more entertaining
than the dreary dead.

Did anyone else hear the screams,
or feel the grief, the anger, the fear,
all of the things I felt there.....

Not One of Us

A small figure at school in
a hot, strange land. The
children left her alone,
she didn't speak their language
or know their games or rules.
She was not one of them.

Winter now and an English
boarding school, where the rules
were known, but not to her.
She was clumsy, wore spectacles,
couldn't tie her tie, dropped the netball,
couldn't master dance steps gracefully
to the music of "Greensleeves",
was not an asset, wouldn't do.
She was not one of them.

She simply asked,
why do the safely-grounded
hear the beat of a terrified heart
and seek to silence it? Is the beat
too loud, something not understood,
something to frighten?
Are things better when the group
destroys the alien in its midst?

She never knew,
she was not one of them.

Sleep Snare

I lie awake and hear
the clock strike three,
and wonder how to
snare elusive sleep,
how to capture it,
how to find
its hiding place
and coax it back to bed.
I might entice it
with crimson berries,
or butter croissants
then pounce on it,
and let it loose
inside my head.
But sharp is cunning sleep
it knows the tricks,
is bored of counting sheep.

I must fly northwards
to the moon
and let sleep take me

soon

          soon

                    soon ....

The Mind Cupboard

My mind cupboard overflows
with unwanted debris.
It needs a spring clean.

I will brush away the cobwebs
of cheerless thoughts.
Scrub out the stains of childhood.

I will replace the brass hooks
corroded with salt tears,
empty all the screams
hoarded through the years.

I will replace the accumulated ashes
from the worn shelf-paper,
with virgin tissue.

I will chase and catch the wasps,
relieve them of their stings.
I will refill this cupboard
with love, and learnt, brighter things.

A Charlbury Voice

"Things were different then," the old chap said,
"Some born and died in the same old bed.
Saddlers, glove makers, and the railroad
gave men jobs; and kept them proud.
Yes, men kept guns but shot to eat,
the poorer families had little other meat.
People helped each other through their lives,
with babies safely born to knowing wives.
Walking through the town you talked to everyone,
no privacy, of course, but things got done.

Now I know or speak to few people here,
and fewer people talk to me, or care,
I hear the railway is just a single track,
and a wilderness overtaking round the back.
Once men worked there selling coal,
later with its disuse, forced on the dole.

Then, useful things were sold in shops.
The ironmonger sold screws, pins, string and mops,
darning needles, hammers, dusters, candles, brown teapots,
measures, light bulbs, garden hoses, children's cots.

On summer evenings children ran down the southern road,
and played and picnicked by the Evenlode.
In those days we wandered, happy, daring, free -
well, nothing now is as it used to be.
Modern life is twisted, the proper order is unsure,
people not content with little, ever wanting more.

There is danger everywhere, from cars and caravans,
litter in the street, discarded bottles, empty cans.
The evening peace with rooks my music overhead,

silenced; a cacophony of noise instead
from pubs, which need the trade, and so
by popular demand silence had to go.

Were people more contented then? It's not for me to say,
and yet I think they seemed so in my day".

The Shed

The spider let himself down
from a crack in the grimy rafters.
Time to spin another web,
catch flies, feed his children.
This old shed he loved
had housed his ancestors,
its essence was in his blood.
He knew well the aged wooden bench
laden with hand-worn tools,
the swallow's yearly nesting place,
the bee's hum and buzz.
He knew of the warmth from the earth floor,
from the hurricane lamp, lit on dark evenings,
of the dusty windows facing north,
and he knew he could swing on the ash spokes
spliced to the wheel hung on the hook.
He knew too that the moonlight
cast quiet shadows on the pile of logs,
home to small scuttling creatures.
He knew that nearby in a bed of shavings,
an old dog slept.
This restful shed scented with lavender and tar,
was a timeless place.

Clearing, cleaning, scraping, peeling,
the old shed becomes new.
Much buzzing and humming
as computers move in, reference books,
filing cabinets, printers, blaring telephones,
glaring lights, and stress.

No quiet shadows now
in the bright new shed,
no cracks, no silence, and the spider.... dead.

England Dear to Me

It is the robins, blackbirds, blue tits,
hopping and grubbing in the garden
that lurch my heart
make England dear to me.
It is the velvet of green moss,
oak trees, old with history,
the first cowslips,
hedgerows filled with dog rose, foxgloves,
and shy sweetpeas in china bowls.
It is finding tea rooms in small market towns,
enticing with homemade scones and strawberry jam,
or suddenly glimpsing church spires
inching their way to heaven.
It is finding a Norman church,
full with a thousand years of prayer,
and a quiet churchyard mothering its dead.
It is small country lanes, high hedged,
views of mauve hills stretching skywards,
sheep and lambs dotting the green,
and bleached Norfolk beaches,
silence only broken with a seagull's cry.
It is the people,
their sense of humour,
their way of saying "sorry" when you bump into them,
their fairness, and once or twice a year
their "letting go",
singing "Jerusalem" with tears and passion.

It is these things
that lurch my heart
make England dear to me.

Invocation to Iona

"Iona, sacred island, mother,
I honour you,
who cradle the
bones of Scottish Kings,
who birthed coloured gemstones
to enchant bleached beaches,
who shelter puffins on your rocks.

I wrap myself in your history,
and knot the garment with
machair rope-grass.
In the Port of Coracle
your southern bay,
I hear the wind-blown cormorant's cry,
and draw a breath.
I see Columba's footsteps
in the sand, and weep.
Tears overflow,
I am spirit-engulfed.

I ask you, Iona,
is this then, or now,
what is, or what has been?
Does the rolling salt sea-mist
cover the uncounted time between?"

Life's Bran Tub

Under a cowl
a glimpsed face,
ploughed with hardship.
A grim mouth,
with broken teeth,
thin and hungry looking,
eyes dull, destined
to assured adversity.

Under a crown of hair,
a glimpsed face,
round and fair,
with milky skin,
bright eyes, white teeth,
and confident smile
of assured security.

Stone

I wrapped the stone in linen cloth,
the picnic I wrapped in plastic bags.
We made for the river the stone and I.
My arm ached with the weight.

We sat on the bank,
watched the river run.

I fed myself tomato sandwiches,
shortbread, spring water.
The stone was still and silent.
I fed it words.

Standing up I said: "Stone
you have been my life companion.
My fetter, me, chained to you.
Hurling you into the river
will be my resurrection".

Two Faces

The wicked wolf tripped
lightly onto the stage,
his ears pricked, his eyes atwinkle.
He wore a yellow waistcoat,
smart tweed breeches,
and to cheerful music he danced
delightfully, tapping his toes,
then, smoothing his whiskers
he sang in a haunting voice
a familiar love song.
And the audience loved him.

He appeared suddenly from nowhere
twirling his handsome brush,
with a pretty girl on his arm.
Grinning widely he made witty jokes,
energy oozed from every pore,
this wolf was Mr. Alive.
And the audience loved him.

On the bus home she sat opposite a man
wearing a shabby raincoat, eyes downcast,
head bent, almost invisible,
almost without the breath of life.
But she recognised him, knew his secret.
Knew he was the wicked wolf
that the audience loved.

Attic Trunk

Searching through her mother's attic trunk
she recognised a dusty, broken cricket bat,
saw a tiny knotted shawl that must have shrunk
and a youthful photo of Aunt Dora, looking fat.
She found silver shoes wrapped in a crimson gypsy skirt
and a purple box housing a worn-thin wedding ring,
a Spanish fan trimmed with lace, and a grandad shirt
embracing faded love letters, tied with ageing string.
From sepia postcards she studied unknown folk,
and pulled out, lovingly, a greasy-tweed cloth cap,
her father's penny whistle, a badger carved from oak,
and brass rubbings, rolled up in a parchment map.
Precious things we keep are candles on our life's tree,
their discovery tells secret stories, provides a key.

Rib-caged Virus

The obscene creature
crouches in its corner.
All at once it leaps
striking out
hurling itself against the rib-boned cage.
Spitting venom-virus
it grasps the throat
twisting, punching, pulling
with fierce, unrelenting strength.
Its slate-black tentacles encircle
its victim's airways,
and squeeze their breath,
as it rattles the bones.
It attacks, attacks again, then
all at once it stills,
slouches, crouches, grins and waits,
tongue lolling.

The woman gasps
at the onslaught,
coughs, croups, sweats, retches,
spits the debris,
feels faint-weary
sleep-deprived, dirty,
exhausted, fearful.

The clock ticks.
The woman waits.

Small Moments of Warmth

I remember a little warmth,
Joey trotting the family through Norfolk lanes,
the small yellow trap swaying in the sunshine.

I remember picnics on Yarmouth beach
with enough blue sky "to make a sailor's trouser".
We ate cucumber sandwiches, Penguin biscuits.

I remember dark evenings,
the small warm flame from a Tilly lamp
lighting the kitchen, and sometimes for supper
we had chicken, chocolate mousse.

I remember a warm holiday in France
squeezed into the back of a car,
singing old thirties love songs.

But will these small moments of warmth,
at the end, be enough to heat and split
the heavy stones that circle the human heart,
allow salt tears to trickle through the cracks?

Chawton Revisited

Do you remember Chawton, Jill,
forty years ago,
discussing Emma, Miss Bates, Fanny?
Do you remember
our mutual dislike of Aunt Norris
and her devious ways?

Do you remember the sitting-room, Jill,
with the round writing table
small, mirror-polished,
set in a garden-view window, or
the satin slippers tied with a ribbon,
the lace collars
embroidered by hand?

Do you remember the walk
to the church in the afternoon cool?
We sat on a bench in the late summer sun,
and mused on her death,
wondering why did she die, so young.

Do you remember Chawton, Jill?

Alone, alive, having tea in the tea room,
I feel you here with me still.

A Curse

on those who plunder the earth,
and violate sacred places......

A curse on those who disturb
and steal gently-bandaged skulls,
legs, arms, and finger-bones,
jewels: perhaps a pearl bracelet,
a coral ring, hair pins, or a mosaic plate,
set out lovingly with food
for the long journey home.
Who have lain there, at peace,
for many thousand years,
the sand, the desert winds, the rains,
nature's bed.

A curse on those whose
laughter and excitement
fills the air, stealing these remains,
transporting them to people
in white coats,
who dissect their dignity,
stick labels on them,
give them to museums
to enlighten an ice-cream-licking public.

Bus Stop Princess

She waited, unnoticed, invisible.
Her fluffy green jersey egg-stained,
uninteresting trousers and sensible shoes
inviting no attention.
She was a brown paper parcel,
loosely string-tied.

But she smiled at me
with such sweetness,
such a smile of goodness,
I saw her sensible shoes
become sparkling slippers,
her shabby clothes
turn into a ball dress
fashioned from sunlight,
stitched up with love.

Not then a story-book princess,
but a real princess
glimpsed at a bus stop.

A Grimsby Fisherman's Wife
Mrs. Ethel Richardson

During the day she knitted
her life into rough wool sweaters.
Fear of north-east gales,
- more forecast -
fear of no return,
and Friday night beatings,
were turned with a collar,
stitched with sober wools.
Knit one, purl one.

Men known to her, sea-taken;
the grief of loss for
a babe or two; and
winter storms and
treacherous rocks that
albatrossed a fisherman's life,
were knitted into sleeves,
into polo necks.
Knit one, purl one.

At night from her narrow bed,
she knitted dreams of exotic places,
warm from the southern sun.
She danced on beaches, cockle-free
and knitted love
into her dream sweaters,
with wools, brightly coloured,
corals, blues, pinks, and red.
By night she knitted pumpkins.
Knit one, pearl one.

No Enquiries

What do enquiries matter?
What do they mean?

She is my mother, damn it,
And they should have been.

Realization

I am
part of the whole.

I am
in the first light,
the bird's first song,
the sun's first dart
through the curtain crack,
in the music of summer trees.

I am
part of the alpha,
the birth,
the awakening,
the growing and spreading,
the throbbing of life.

I am part of all suffering
hands blood-stained.
Part of the love
humanity shares and
of all good things.

I am
part of the omega,
the closing, the last light,
the call back from the dark
to the bright, eternal night.

Word-dancing

The woman discovers the double act
of word-dancing at dinner,
recognizes with excitement
mutual friends from books, from poetry,
from worlds explored, but only
known thus far in solitude.

Together they dance through imagined lands
sharing knowledge,
throwing words back and forth
in light ethereal movements,
cerebral binding and bonding,
now the foxtrot, now the waltz.

For her these pleasures
are found at lunch parties, at dinner,
in libraries, on courses.
But where can the young word-dance?
Her grandson lunches on the run,
dines with Eastenders,
goes clubbing on solitary trips
too noisy, frightening, for word-dancing,
for cerebral binding and bonding,
now the foxtrot, now the waltz.

Soldier's Meditation

My cigarette time-burns,
my body trembles,
only minutes now
until the action starts.

Am I brave? No, not brave
I am shit-scared,
my body reeks.
The last drop of whisky
wets my parched lips.
I light another cigarette.

I hold this gun to hide behind.
With it, I will aim and slaughter
someone unknown, someone's son,
mother, father, daughter.

If killed, I want no part in bands playing,
or speeches glorifying my sacrifice.
I want no weeping, seen or unseen,
pitying those who were,
those who had been.

Go, action, ready, time to start.
Dear God, do leaden wings always fly
a universal soldier's heart?

Universal Truth

Everyone knows
that Philip Larkin wrote:

"They fuck you up,
your mum and dad,
they may not mean to,
but they do".

And what Philip Larkin knew,
I know to be true.

Bridal Red

I saw
a young girl smiling,
laughing, threading beads, minding goats,
chasing chickens, pulling feathers from their tails,
holding hands with sisters, friends,
chattering, gossiping, rough and tumbling
in bright sunlight.

I saw
scrub-plains, white rocks and blue,
blue mountains, straw huts,
men on haunches, chewing,
and thin dogs, fat babies,
loving families, happiness.

I saw
men, suddenly, appear from a distant village,
offering cows and sheep as an exchange
for a shepherd in need of a woman, a wife.
The girl was chosen,
a bargain was struck.

I saw
her stand silently, acquiescent,
red ochre paste and mud
plastered on her shaven head,
necklaces of golden wire
wound tightly round her neck,
ankle bracelets in profusion.

I saw
her sisters, her friends, not laughing now,
offering presents,

a carved stick, a beaded purse.
At dawn she would leave as the sun rose,
to walk over the mountain pass
to an unknown bridegroom,
an unknown life.

I saw
as she left
her grief, her tears trickling,
then flooding through the paste and mud.
I saw her sorrow as the colour red,
and a crown of thorns her maidenhead.